# What Kinda CACTUS Izzat?

A "WHO'S WHO" OF STRANGE PLANTS
IN THE SOUTHWESTERN AMERICAN DESERT

by REG·MANNING

CARTOONS BY THE AUTHOR

Reganson
CARTOON BOOKS
PHOENIX, ARIZONA

# What Kinda Cactus Izzat?

## PRINTING HISTORY

SIX EDITIONS PUBLISHED BY
J.J. AUGUSTIN, INC., NEW YORK
FIRST EDITION, DECEMBER 1941
SECOND PRINTING, MARCH 1942
THIRD PRINTING, FEBRUARY 1944
FOURTH PRINTING, JANUARY 1945
FIFTH PRINTING, MARCH 1946
SIXTH PRINTING, SEPTEMBER 1949
EDITIONS PUBLISHED BY
REGANSON CARTOON BOOKS, PHOENIX, ARIZONA
SEVENTH PRINTING, SEPTEMBER 1953
EIGHTH PRINTING, OCTOBER 1957
*(Slightly revised)*
NINTH PRINTING, AUGUST 1958
TENTH PRINTING, FEBRUARY 1960
ELEVENTH PRINTING, FEBRUARY 1961
TWELFTH PRINTING, MARCH 1962
THIRTEENTH PRINTING, FEBRUARY 1963
FOURTEENTH PRINTING, DECEMBER 1963
*(Illustrations slightly revised)*
FIFTEENTH PRINTING, NOVEMBER 1964
SIXTEENTH PRINTING, FEBRUARY 1966
SEVENTEENTH PRINTING, FEBRUARY 1967
EIGHTEENTH PRINTING, MAY 1968
NINETEENTH PRINTING, MARCH 1969
*(Copyright renewed December 1969)*
TWENTIETH PRINTING, FEBRUARY 1970
TWENTY-FIRST PRINTING, JANUARY 1971
TWENTY-SECOND PRINTING, AUGUST 1971
TWENTY-THIRD PRINTING, APRIL 1972
TWENTY-FOURTH PRINTING, JANUARY 1973
TWENTY-FIFTH PRINTING, DECEMBER 1973
TWENTY-SIXTH PRINTING, APRIL 1975
TWENTY-SEVENTH PRINTING, MARCH 1976
TWENTY-EIGHTH PRINTING, MAY 1977
TWENTY-NINTH PRINTING, MAY 1978
THIRTIETH PRINTING, MAY 1979
THIRTY-FIRST PRINTING, JANUARY 1981
THIRTY-SECOND PRINTING, MAY 1982
THIRTY-THIRD PRINTING, FEBRUARY 1984
THIRTY-FOURTH PRINTING, APRIL 1985
THIRTY-FIFTH PRINTING, APRIL 1987
THIRTY-SIXTH PRINTING, OCTOBER 1989
THIRTY-SEVENTH PRINTING, FEBRUARY 1992

# CONTENTS

# INTRODUCTION

# THE CACTUS BELT

The U. S.-Mexican border is one region which should never have to worry about an invasion by parachutists. It would be hard to choose a territory in the world less suited for haphazard dropping in on. North of the border, from Texas to California, is the cactus belt of the United States, where nearly every native plant, even the lily, comes armed with needles, knives, or swords. South of the border is the same, only more so. (See map, pages 68-69)

Floating down by parachute, you might be tempted to steer for a landing in one of those patches which look like a bed of thistle down. This would be a mistake! The "thistle down" is the sheep's clothing of one of the orneriest species of cacti — the Cholla (CHAW-yuh) "jumping" cactus. There is some debate whether this plant actually jumps on its victims; there is no debate at all about the victims jumping.

No, the Mexican borderland is definitely not the best strategic spot for setting down, via parachute or otherwise. It isn't even adviseable to bend over, without first looking behind you.

1

# DESERT DEFENSE PLANTS

Human kind might learn a lesson of survival from the cactus. It conserves its resources and arms to the teeth. In a land where every drop of water is contested for (by states as well as plants) the cactus not only gets its share of moisture, but manages to store up reserve supplies to withstand years of scarcity. It never goes looking for trouble, but it can dish out plenty of misery to anybody who tries to push it around.

Not only cacti, but almost everything that survives in the Southwest desert has to scratch for a living. Just because a plant has thorns, that's no sign it's a cactus. Even if some folks call it a cactus, it aint necessarily so. Big plants, little plants — trees and bushes — all have thorns.

Desert thorns are not used exclusively as weapons. Sometimes they serve as means of transportation. If a joint of cactus latches on to your person, it may only be hitching a ride. When you dislodge it at a more or less distant place, the cactus joint will take root and grow into a new plant.

When you visit the desert, pursue a middle course — don't throw your weight around, don't try to get too chummy — just keep hands off the plants and you won't get hurt.

— EVEN THE
LILIES CARRY
SWORDS —

3

.... LEFT OVER
FROM SOME
PREHISTORIC
AGE.

# THE DESERT IN BLOOM

Many people, visiting the Southwest desert for the first time, expect to see a sandy waste something like the Sahara. Instead, they find a land that is more like a botanical garden. Spread over thousands of square miles of valleys and plateaus, the vast desert floor is covered with an even layer of egg-sized rocks. Jagged "cardboard" mountains, like stage sets in the light of desert dawn and dusk, make a background for the display of weird foliage which seems to have been left over from some prehistoric age.

In Arizona and southward into old Mexico the desert becomes a riot of plant life. In some places it is almost jungle thick — you'd need an axe to force your way through. But most surprising thing to many visitors is the desert in bloom. Cactus blossoms are as colorful as tulips—as delicate as orchids. Some open up during the daylight hours — others appear only in the black of night. And the other desert plants are lavish in their display of floral beauty, too. All have the ability to bloom even in the driest years. In an occasional rainy springtime wild flowers blanket the desert floor and mountainsides in a blaze of color.

# TONGUE TWISTERS

Neomammillaria microcarpa, echinocactus xeranthemoides, opuntia phaeacantha, coryphantha muehlenpfordtii. Those are not names of new wonder drugs, or this year's All-American football team. They are the names which botanists call various kinds of cacti. They call 'em that to keep from getting 'em mixed up with the Fouquieriaceae, which also grows on the desert. Before you return this book to the store, we hasten to assure you that we shall make no attempt in this opus to regale you with the scientific classification of desert plants. We shall try to introduce you to outstanding citizens of the region, and describe 'em so you can recognize a cactus when you run into one (if you're interested at the time) but we're not contracting to give you a post graduate course in Latin. If it's an education you're after, why didn't you study while you were in school?

The first part of this book will be devoted to the different kinds of cacti (or call 'em cactuses if you prefer). In the back of the book we'll point out other desert plants, many of which are often erroneously called "cactus". Actually some of these plants are much more closely related to an onion than they are to a cactus.

# THE CACTUS CLAN

The next time you sit in a clump of cactus, examine the needles carefully as you remove them. You will notice that the needles don't just grow out of the wall of the cactus—each cactus has special little warts, or pincushions, to hold its stickers. You can tell what group of cacti stabbed you by studying these warts.

Every cactus in the Southwest belongs to, or is closely related to one of two principal groups — the OPUNTIA or the CEREUS. The Opuntia cacti have little tufts of "hair" growing along the top of each wart— a patch of tiny stickers often as fine as peach fuzz. Sometimes an Opuntia will not have any full sized thorns at all — but it will have fuzz-stickers on the wart. You can feel them when they get in your finger, but often they are so fine you can hardly see to get 'em out.

The Cereus cacti and their cousins have no hair on their warts — they are absolutely bald. Mebbe that's why they are so cereus. Hm-m-m.

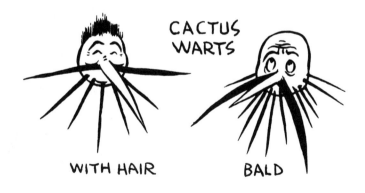

CACTUS WARTS

WITH HAIR          BALD

# PLATES AND CYLINDERS

In case you feel self-conscious about going around stroking cactus warts to see if they have any hair on 'em, there is another way you can tell an Opuntia-type cactus without personal contact. An Opuntia (pronounced oh-PUNCHA) is a jointed plant — made up of segments linked together to form a "chain". There are two branches of the Opuntia family; the Prickly Pears and the Chollas. In the Prickly Pears the links are made up of a series of discs or "plates", one growing out of another. In the Cholla family (which includes all of the "jumping" varieties) the segments are cylinders, joined like link sausage.

There is another essential difference between Prickly Pears and Cholla — their fruit. The fruit of the Pricklies is good to eat when ripe; that of a Cholla — ugh!

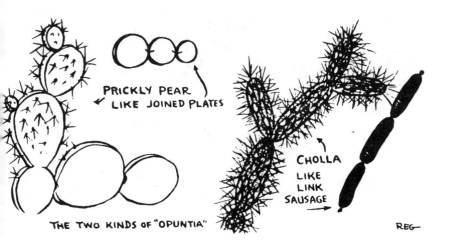

PRICKLY PEAR
LIKE JOINED PLATES

CHOLLA
LIKE
LINK
SAUSAGE

THE TWO KINDS OF "OPUNTIA"

REG

THE PRICKLIES

# THE PRICKLY PEARS

Prickly Pears grow native in every state except Maine, Vermont and New Hampshire. So, though you may never have seen any other kind of a cactus, the chances are you know what a Prickly Pear looks like. Of course, there are dozens of different varieties of Prickly Pears — some with big "beaver tail" segments and others ranging in size down to little Pricklies whose joints are no bigger than your ear. Some varieties string along the ground like a chain of elephants and others fan upward like some kind of hot water bottle display. But by and large, when you've seen one Prickly Pear, you've seen 'em all.

Prickly Pears are the most short-lived of all cacti. They seldom live more than 20 years. But young "plates" may break off of the dying plant, take root and develop a new plant. Under favorable conditions they grow fast and spread all over the landscape.

Most varieties of Prickly Pears have yellow blossoms, though some are red or purple.

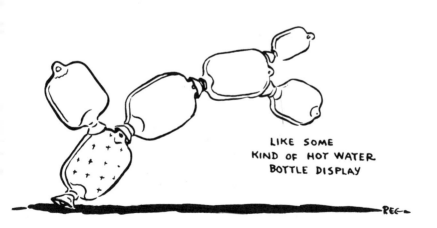

LIKE SOME
KIND OF HOT WATER
BOTTLE DISPLAY

13

# CHAW YUH

CHAW-yuh — that's how you pronounce Cholla — and that's what they do to you upon the slightest provocation — CHAW yuh! Without qualification, the Cholla breed gets our award as the most-unpleasant-cactus-of-the-month-to-sit-on. The Cholla family takes in all of the "cylinder-jointed" varieties of cactus, whose segments range in size from links no bigger than a pencil to some that are as fat as a baloney. But in the Southwest, when you hear anyone speak (bitterly) of a Cholla, he is usually referring to one of the so-called "jumping" varieties.

Cholla blossoms come in almost every conceivable shade with the accent on yellows and reds. Chollas are found throughout the cactus belt and push northward, thinning out and diminishing in size, into Nevada, Utah, Colorado and tips of Oklahoma and Kansas.

# JUMPING CACTUS

A jumping cactus cannot jump — all evidence to the contrary notwithstanding. It is simply a painful illusion — the thorn is quicker than the thigh.

The jumping Cholla is covered with a mass of thistle-white needles that appear soft and harmless. But barely brush against 'em and they attach to you. The joints of the Cholla are so loosely attached that, in the resulting activity, a whole section may break loose and come with you. The victim of the jumping cactus may not realize that he has even touched the plant until he feels it take hold. When he comes to earth, he may be some distance from the offending plant — and, invariably, he will swear that the piece sticking to him JUMPED across the intervening space to make the attack.

Masses of broken off joints litter the ground around a jumping cactus, waiting to sabotage a passing ankle. These take root and grow. The passing animal or human who carries away a section of Cholla with him thus becomes the unwilling spreader of the plant.

# TEDDY BEAR CHOLLA

Two species of Cholla have about even claim to the nickname of "jumping cactus". The "Teddy Bear" is the smaller, more innocent looking of the two. It is about the "stickeriest" of all cacti, but each of its thousands of needles is encased in a sheath that looks like white tissue. The sun glistening on these white spines makes it appear to be wearing a halo (which it decidedly is NOT) and results in the thistle down effect which gives it the Teddy Bear title.

The Teddy Bear seldom grows more than shoulder high. It has a trunk as big as your wrist, with baloney sized branches, and joints like short frankfurters.

The broken-off pieces which litter the ground around any Cholla are particularly formidable in the case of a Teddy Bear. Even when they die without taking root, the stickers retain their effectiveness. Pack rats and other small desert rodents use 'em to build fortifications around their nests. And tiny flowers live in security among the fallen thorns.

# CHAIN FRUIT CHOLLA

The Fulgida or "chain fruit" Cholla is the second species commonly referred to as a "jumping cactus". It is one of several "tree-Chollas" which reach huge size. The Fulgida sometimes grows 12 feet high with a 12 foot spread of stickery branches.

The astonishing thing about this Cholla is not its size, however, but its fruits. Its fruit has fruit! The fruit never ripens, but hangs on the plant until the next season, when new fruit grows right out of the end of last year's crop. This process continues year after year, forming long chains of hanging fruit which finally get so heavy that they fall off. The fallen fruit takes root — and a new plant is born.

CHAINS OF CHOLLA FRUIT

A STAGHORN

# THE STAGHORNS

Except for the "jumping Cacti", the "staghorns" are the most familiar members of the Cholla tribe. The staghorns are tree-Cholla, as big as the Fulgida jumping cactus, but their branches are skinnier and much less spiny. Staghorns include several varieties of Cholla which can be told apart only by an expert.

If you come across the skeleton branch of a dead staghorn Cholla, you will have no difficulty figuring how it got its nickname. Without its covering of "flesh" and stickers, the dried branch is a pretty good replica of a deer's antlers—both in size and shape. The skeletons of all Cholla trunks and branches are shot through with a network of holes as though somebody had been working on 'em with a machine gun. These porous, woody "mailing tubes" are widely used in the manufacture of small novelty furniture — floor lamps, picture frames, etc. They take an excellent polish and the Swiss cheese effect is interesting.

# CEREUS BUSINESS

A clan of spiny specters — everything from giants with arms 15 feet long to little fellows cringing under desert brush — make up the Cereus family. The majestic Saguaro is king of the breed — and the scrawny Night Blooming Cereus, who never plays its tuber, is at once the most insignificant and spectacular member of the family. As a matter of fact, all the true Cereus Cacti are night blooming, but the one that bears that name is the most widely known of the species. Being small, it has been domesticated as a potted plant.

A host of other cacti are cousins of the Cereus (according to "informed sources"). There's the Barrel cactus family — water tanks o' th' desert; the low-down Hedgehogs; the "Pineapples" (this is our own designation, so don't go asking any scientists about it — they haven't heard of 'em yet by that name); and there are the inch-high Pincushions — a Giant Saguaro could hold a score of 'em in his shoe. The Saguaro, incidentally, really does have shoes . . . wooden shoes.

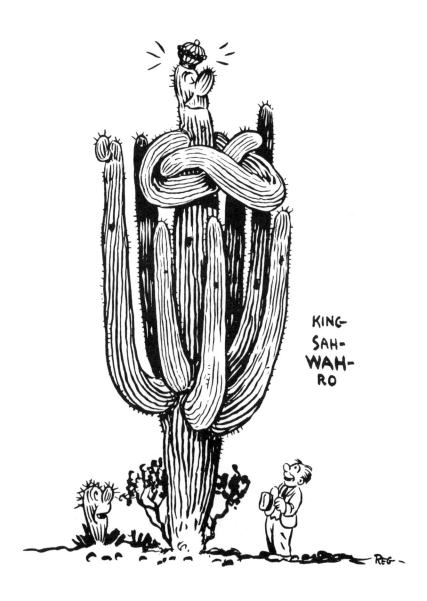

KING-
SAH-
WAH-
RO

# LORD OF THE DESERT

Great grandpappy of the Cactus Clan — undisputed Lord of the Southwest Desert — that is the Giant Saguaro. The Saguaro (pronounced sah-WAH-ro) outranks all others both in size and longevity. Full grown, it stands 50 feet high — and it lives a couple of centuries.

The Giant Cactus grows slowly — as befits a monarch. At the age of 10 years it may be no bigger than an ostrich egg — though it already has whiskers; at the age of 21 it may stand as high as a draftee, but it is little more than an infant in the Saguaro world; at 75 the Giant is probably 12 feet tall and may even have started to grow its arms; at full maturity of 200 it will "rare" up to 50 feet and salute you with three or four dozen arms.

# DANCING GIANTS

Driving through a Saguaro forest for the first time makes you feel a little self-conscious. The Giants stand about in groups, by twos or threes, or by dozens, silent, but all watching you. It's like walking into a crowded room, where everybody stops what he is doing and waits in embarrassed silence till you have passed through. The larger Giants, with their dozens of twisted arms, seem to have been "frozen" in the midst of some wild dance-orgy. Others huddle together as though they had been caught gossiping about YOU.

The Saguaro lives in Arizona, sometimes in forests which cover the hills as far as the eye can see. They also grow south of the border in Old Mexico. A scattering few spill across the Colorado River into California. In Mexico and South America there are other species of cereus, similar in size and appearance to the Saguaro. One of these, the Indian Comb Cereus, grows profusely along Mexico's Gulf of California, and is often mistaken for a Saguaro. But instead of juicy red fruit, it has fruits so dry and spiny, the Indians use them to groom their hair. Hence the name.

To see one of the finest stands of Saguaro Giants, visit Saguaro National Monument near Tucson, Arizona.

FALLEN
GIANT—
A BUNDLE OF
STICKS—

REC-

# A COLUMN OF WATER

The Saguaro is Nature's engineering marvel. Built along lines which Man employs only in the most modern of reenforced concrete, the Giant Cactus is also equipped with an automatic plumbing system.

Find the skeleton of a dead Saguaro on the desert, and you will see that the trunk and arms are formed by cylinders of woody "fish-pole" rods — exactly like the framework you would make of steel bars if you were building a round concrete post. Into and around this framework is "poured" the pulp of the plant, which is just as wet and about the color of the white meat of a watermelon rind. A Saguaro is about 98% water. The skin of the cactus reminds you of that of a watermelon, too, but it is tougher and a lighter green.

SECTION OF A SAGUARO
CUT AWAY TO SHOW
FRAMEWORK OF
RODS —

REC-

# LIVING TELEPHONE POLES

If you have never seen a Saguaro it is hard to visualize just how big an engineering job it is for Nature to set one of 'em up. To get an idea of the size and shape of one, imagine a telephone pole 50 feet high and two feet thick at the base, with 12 or more poles of varying sizes branching from it candelabra fashion. That would make a pretty good life-sized wooden model of a Saguaro. The weight of the telephone-pole-model would probably be about the same as that of the real thing, too. With its water-logged pulp, a Saguaro that big would probably weigh 10 to 15 tons.

All this immense tower of weight is supported by a mat of "woven" roots set only a few inches under the surface of the ground, but the cactus is held aloft as firmly as a broomstick inserted in the hub of a bicycle wheel.

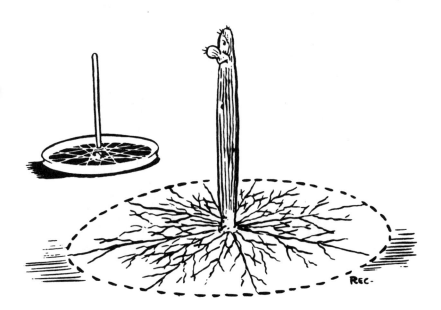

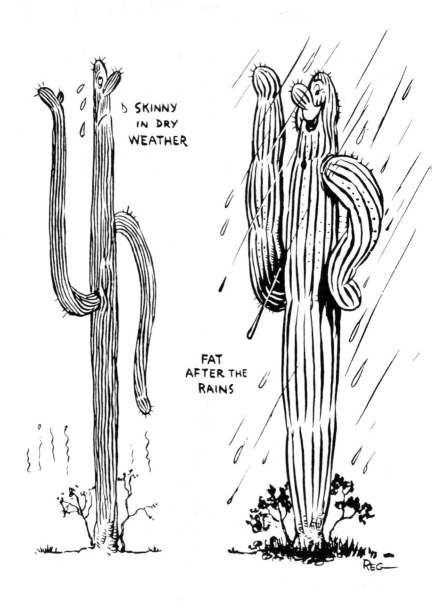

# SAGUARO PLUMBING SYSTEM

At the base of a Giant Saguaro the "fish poles" of the skeleton grow together to form a solid, woody hub. From this hub the shallow roots extend like interlaced wire spokes. The roots of a 50-foot cactus will reach 65 feet in every direction from the plant.

The roots and rods form the plumbing system of the Saguaro. When it rains, the network of roots sponges up water at full speed and pumps it to the plant, where it is quickly distributed to every section of the cactus. In this way the cactus can pump and store, during one rainy season, enough water to last four years without another drink. And throughout the four years it will bloom and bear fruit regularly. That's got a camel beat by plenty.

Corrugated ridges follow the fish-pole ribs from top to bottom of the trunk and branches. As water is stored in the Saguaro, it swells and these ridges pull further apart — like an accordion. Then as the water is used up during dry weather the plant gets gaunt, while the accordion-ridges fold close together.

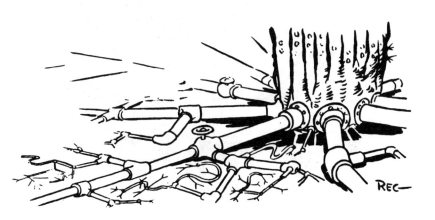

# CACTUS CAVES

There are caves inside Giant Cacti—with living inhabitants! In nearly every Saguaro you will notice a number of round holes. These were not made by the tin-horn "hunters" who so frequently shoot up our road signs. They are the doorways of woodpecker caves. A little desert woodpecker will drill through the "rind" of the cactus till he disappears into the interior. Inside he hollows out a room and sets up housekeeping. Next year he will not return to the old home — he'll dig himself a new cave in some other cactus.

After the woodpeckers move out, other small birds take out a second mortgage — without references or co-signers — and move into the ready-made apartment. The little "elf" owl, no bigger than a sparrow, particularly enjoys the cactus-caves so convenientlly provided without effort on his part.

SHOES

# CACTUS WITH SHOES

If you need further proof that the Saguaro is about the strangest plant in creation, consider the fact that it "wears" shoes to keep from getting dry.

When a Saguaro is injured, a cork-like scar-tissue forms over the wound, which prevents the moisture from seeping out of the plant. Thus, when a woodpecker hollows out a cave inside the cactus, nature goes to work and coats the walls of the little room with "cork-plaster".

Among the ribs of a fallen Saguaro skeleton you will usually see several "wooden shoes" entangled among the ribs. These are the "cork-plaster" caves of the woodpeckers after the pulp of the plant has disintegrated from around them. In shape and size they are often very good replicas of real wooden shoes, though it is doubtful whether you will ever find your exact fit.

Under ordinary conditions, the Saguaro is as tough as it is big. But during a rainy spell, even a small scratch may cause the plant to bleed to death. Woodpeckers know this by instinct, but the human-being-with-a-jacknife sometimes murders a 100-year-old plant to carve his initials.

# SAGUARO FLOWERS AND FRUIT

During the cool desert nights of May the tip of every Saguaro branch is covered with wax-white flowers. Shaped like the end of a bugle, they open up to about the size of a teacup. Best time to see them is in the cool of early morning. By mid-day the blossom will close. It will never reopen. The Saguaro blossom is the official state flower of Arizona.

Saguaro flowers are succeeded by purple fruit. It ripens in mid-summer, and splits open to reveal the bright red fruit-pulp. At this stage it is often mistaken for red blossoms. The ripe fruit is a favorite food of all desert birds. The Indians have harvested it for centuries, using dead Saguaro ribs to reach it. They eat the fruit raw; preserved; or dried, like figs. They also crush the black seeds into a nutritious flour.

Natives of the desert, from prehistoric cliff dwellers to the reservation Indians of today, have made use of Saguaro rib-poles in their dwellings.

THE
HARVEST

THE
ORGAN
PIPE

# THE ORGAN PIPE

The Organ Pipe Cactus, or Pitahaya, like the Saguaro, is a true Cereus, but it is a lot more scarce in the United States than its Giant brother. A single "pipe" of the Organ Pipe might easily be mistaken for a Sagauro branch, but it's not hard to tell the difference between the full grown plants. Where the Saguaro is a "tree", with the branches curving out of a massive trunk, the Organ Pipe is a huge "bush," branching at the ground, without a trunk or predominating central stem. It is made up entirely of "branches". The Organ Pipe Cactus looks like a gigantic many-legged spider lying on its back, with the long curved legs pointing skyward.

The Spidery branches of the Organ Pipe are a lot skinnier than those of the Saguaro, though much more numerous. The plant grows about half as tall as the Giant Cactus, but its bush-like construction causes it to spread out a lot farther.

The Pitahaya Organ Pipe is native to only one locality in the U. S.— an area included, for the most part, within the borders of Organ Pipe National Monument, south of Ajo, Arizona. However, the Desert Botanical Garden of Arizona, near Tempe, has some very fine transplanted specimens. And you'll find it growing in profusion in Old Mexico, a few miles south of Nogales, Arizona.

LIKE
A SPIDER
ON ITS
BACK

# PIPES AND FLOWERS

The Organ Pipe Cactus has one particularly interesting feature — injury causes it to get bigger. If the frost of a chill desert night nips the tender growing tip of an Organ Pipe branch, that stem will stop growing — and a new "pipe" will branch out from the old one. Thus it is that in the northernmost part of its range, where you'd naturally expect the plant to be more scrawny, you will often find Organ Pipes with more branches than in the milder sections to the south.

Like the Saguaro, the Organ Pipe is a night bloomer, but its flower can't compare in beauty. The petals are greenish-white with perhaps a tinge of purple, and never open wide. The fruit of the Organ Pipe is covered with needles, but these brush off easily when it is ripe. They're no worse to get at than a bony fish. The Indians, whose diet has never included enough sugar to suit them, have long prized the very sweet fruit of the Organ Pipe.

45

THE
OLD MAN

# THE OLD MAN CACTUS

If you drive down into old Mexico you will see lots of Senita, or "Old Man" cacti. Only a few specimens of this plant grow wild in the United States (in Southwestern Arizona), but you will see them transplanted in Southwestern cactus gardens.

The Old Man is Cereus — but differs in appearance from both the Saguaro and Organ Pipe. It is "bushy" in construction, but smaller than the Organ Pipe. Whereas both Saguaro and Organ Pipe have accordion-pleated ridges set close together, the Old Man's ridges are widely separated "flanges" running from top to bottom of the branches. The cross section of a sliced-through branch would make a six or seven-pointed star, while the cross section of Saguaro or Organ Pipe would form a many-pointed cog-wheel.

Like all other Cereus cacti, the Old Man puts out its pink blossom at night. The flowers grow down along the side of the plant. And, confidentially — well, they are NOT sweet smelling.

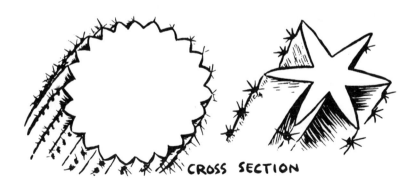

CROSS SECTION

THREE CEREUS GUYS

# THE OLD MAN HAS WHISKERS

"Old Man" Senita has one feature we have never seen on any other cactus. It has swinging roots. These little roots hang on the elbows of the upturning branches — swinging in mid-air above the ground — and look for all the world like straggling goatee-whiskers. When the weight of a branch causes it to bend or break and touch the ground, the whisker-roots will dig in and take up the active duty for which roots were intended. It is this feature of the Senita which causes it to spread, forming bush-clumps, rather than the single bush formation of the Organ Pipe.

Thorns on most of the plant, particularly on the younger branches, are short spikes. But at the top of the older branches the spines turn into matted white bristles that look like gray hair — which gives it the name of Senita (say-NEET-as), or "senile" Old Man.

# NIGHT BLOOMING CEREUS

Most desert plants rely for protection on their formidable armament of needles, spikes and "swords". The Night Blooming Cereus specializes in camouflage. You can walk close enough to one to touch it, and never see it. Growing under desert shrubs, the scrawny stems of the Night Bloomers look like nothing more than a few dead sticks. Don't waste your time rushing around the desert looking for the Night Blooming Cereus — it's harder to find than parking space in a one-hour zone. Your best bet for seeing it is at one of the Southwestern cactus gardens.

Its habit of growing underneath bushes, besides serving as a camouflage, also keeps it from being trampled. It usually grows only about two feet high, and its stems are brittle near the base, so this is no small danger. Along the ribs of its skinny (less than an inch thick) stems, the stickers of the Night Bloomer are not much protection — they are less than an eighth of an inch long.

# QUEEN OF THE NIGHT

To the Night Blooming Cereus, most scrawny, helpless, good-for-nothing looking plant of the desert, goes our blue ribbon and the "AH-H-H" award for most beautiful flower in the cactus world. The blossom is a GORGEOUS many pointed white star — a star that outshines those in the heavens. Just after dusk in late May or June, the flower starts opening in a series of spasmodic jerks. It gives off a heavy, sweet fragrance that can be detected half a block away. Fully open the star is as big as a saucer. Early the following morning, after one night of glory, it closes up, never to open again.

The potted Night Blooming Cereus which you may have grown in your living room, was probably a foreigner transplanted from some tropical Latin-American country. The Southwestern variety is native to West Texas, New Mexico and Arizona.

# BULB FOR THE NIGHT BLOOMER

The Night Blooming Cereus stores its juice in a bulb underground. The desert has a never-ending supply of surprises. While the Giant Saguaro is supported by an apparently flimsy net of shallow roots, the insignificant Night Bloomer has a huge tuberous root. The tuber is kind of an overgrown turnip. Overgrown is right — the "turnip" of one Night Bloomer weighed in at more than 100 pounds. Ordinarily they vary in weight from two to 45 pounds. These "turnips" serve as storage tanks for the Cereus' water supply. The big bulbs actually taste like turnips, too — Indians slice 'em and fry 'em in deep fat.

The bright red fruit of a Night Bloomer is good to eat, too, if you can find it. (The birds usually find it first.) The flowers furnish nectar for insects. Attracted by the fragrances, they flock in on blooming night to get a drink — and, incidentally, to help in the pollination of the plant.

THE
BARRELS

# THE BARRELS

Don't hate yourself if, your first time on the desert, you mistake a Barrel Cactus for a baby Giant Saguaro. A six-foot Saguaro, just getting started in life, really looks a lot like a full grown Barrel. If you will examine the spines, however, you will be able to tell 'em apart easily enough. A Saguaro has straight, white "darning needles", while the Barrel is armed with flat, red spikes, as long as your finger and cruelly hooked at the end. At a little distance the Saguaro will appear naked of thorns; the thickly interlaced hooks of the Barrel gives it the appearance of being wrapped in heavy mesh.

Species of Barrel Cacti make up a large desert family, ranging in size from little "kegs", a few inches high, to huge "drums" 10 feet tall. They are found in Texas, New Mexico, Arizona and California.

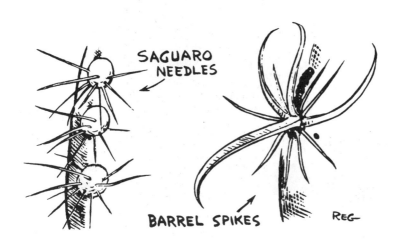

# DESERT LIFE SAVER

"Bisnaga" (bees-NAH-gah), the Spaniards called the Barrel Cacti—and in their language that meant "barrel". Translated into English, the name has stuck. In the days before the filling station and the soda pop stand, the Barrel Cactus was a life saver to desert wanderers. The old timer with an empty canteen used to hack the top off a waist high Bisnaga and tamp the white meat with a stick. Then scooping up handfuls of the resulting mush, he squeezed out the water and threw away the pulp. Soon the scooped out hole would be partially fillled with milky water — something like the vegetable juice so popular as a health drink today. We have no records as to its vitamin content, but it did quench the traveler's thirst. And it certainly left his hands a good deal cleaner.

The Barrel Cactus served the desert wanderer in still another way—it acted as a compass. The Bisnaga nearly always leans a little to the south.

# THE CANDY KID

The "cactus candy", which you find on sale in the Southwest, is made from the pulp of the Barrel Cactus. This often gives folks the false idea that the Bisnaga is full of "syrup", like a maple tree. Actually in the manufacture of cactus candy, the white meat is cut in squares and boiled in water to remove all the sap. Then it is boiled in sugar syrup to produce the confection, which turns out almost exactly like the watermelon preserves mother (or grandma) used to make.

Each summer the Barrels put on beautiful floral bonnets — red-orange or yellow blossoms that form in a ring on the tip-top of the cactus. You won't have to lose any sleep to see 'em, either, 'cause they bloom in the daytime.

BARREL
BLOSSOMS
ON
TOP

THE HEDGEHOGS

# THE HEDGEHOGS

Squatting close to the ground and huddled together, a clump of Hedgehog Cacti resembles a squad of little porcupines with quills set for action. Like the Barrels, the Hedgehog family includes many species which produce a bewildering variety of blossoms — flowers with thick waxy petals — and flowers as delicate as an orchid.

Most of the dill pickle-shaped Hedgehogs have bristles that look very much like those of Cholla jumping cacti. They grow in small groups of two or three "pickles", or in vast clumps containing hundreds of members.

Hedgehogs are "wanderers" — you'll find 'em in the desert — or in the mountains, crouching in the shade of the oak trees. They are found throughout the cactus belt states.

Most spectacular of the Hedgehogs is the Rainbow cactus. Collectors have practically denuded the desert of this variety, but you can see it in Southwest cactus gardens. The stickers, lying flat against the plant, form in different colored bands — red, white, yellow, etc., — around the plant, marking each year's growth. These colored bands give the Rainbow its name.

THE RAINBOW

# THE PINCUSHION

Pincushion cacti are midgets of the Cactus world. One of the tiniest of the Pincushions has a botanical name a mile long — Neomammillaria microcarpia. (Mebbe you oughta memorize that to recite to your friends on dull evenings. "On the desert," you can say, "I sat down beside a neo-mammy-laria micro-carpa . . .") As for us we'll just call it a Pincushion — we can't say, "Neomamm - mamm -" — oh HECK!

The Pincushion looks like an egg encased in a course woolen jacket, decorated with black fishhooks. The "wool" is formed by a mass of fine stickers covering the cactus so completely that it seems to be white. Out of this thatch protrude the black-brown spines that look just like fishhooks.

Pincushions grow all over the desert country. If you buy one of those little souvenir boxes of dwarf cacti in a Southwestern gift shop you'll be sure to find at least one Pincushion included.

The tiniest of pincushions puts out blossoms as big as much larger cacti. Sometimes the flowers look bigger than the plant itself.

# THE "PINEAPPLES"

The "Pineapples" is our own nickname for a group of cacti which the "experts" usually classify as "Coryphantha" (cory-FAN-tha) — a name which is much too fanthy for us. They are so closely related to the "Neomammillaria" Pincushions, that both often are lumped under the same Pincushion nickname. Our "Pineapple" cactus has a criss-cross pattern, dividing it into a series of lumps — each lump studded with a rosette of thorns. In the smaller varieties, the effect is very similar to the Pincushions we have described, but in larger plants the criss-cross pattern, their size and shape make them look a lot like a real pineapple. The Pincushions have these lumps too, but their thatch covers 'em so completely you'd never know it. In the several varieties of smaller Pineapples and larger Pincushions, which so closely resemble each other, scientists tell 'em apart by getting down and examining these lumps. If the lump has a little groove in the top of it, the cactus is a "Coryphantha" Pineapple — if it's smooth, it's a "Neomammillaria" pincushion.

The "Pineapples" wear their flowers like a hat — large yellow or pink blossoms growing right on top.

America's Desert Garden

THE CACTUS

AMERICA'S DESERT GARDEN *alo*

CORTEZ

Pincushions

COLORADO

DODGE CITY

Prickly Pears

KANS.

OKLAHOMA

NEW MEXICO

SANTA FE

Yucca

AMARILLO

66

ALBUQUERQUE

60

Hedgehogs

87

YUCCA BLOSSOM STATE FLOWER

85

70

Barrels

180

Yuccas

WHITE SANDS N.M.

CARLSBAD CAVERN N.M.

CARLSBAD

.W. RESEARCH STA. AM. MUSEUM of NAT. HIST.

EL PASO

TEXAS

JUAREZ

Pincushions

80

290

TO MEXICO CITY

Prickly Pears

BIG BEND NAT'L PARK

Chollas

Night Bloomers

90

DEL RIO

REG·MANNING

ELT

the MEXICAN BORDER

# "CACTUSES" THAT ARE NOT CACTI

Most people make the mistake of calling everything on the desert "cactuses". The "Monkey Tail Cactus" and the "Spanish Dagger Cactus", f'rinstance, are not cacti at all. They are as different, botanically, from a cactus, as a scallion. A Spanish Dagger is, in fact, a lot more closely related to garlic than it is to the Cactus Family. So far, in this book, we have tried to give you a speaking acquaintance with the leaders of the Cactus Clan. Now we'll turn our attention to other thorny plants which, while they are NOT cacti, are just as odd. No cactus is more "typical" of the desert than the queer breeds you are about to meet.

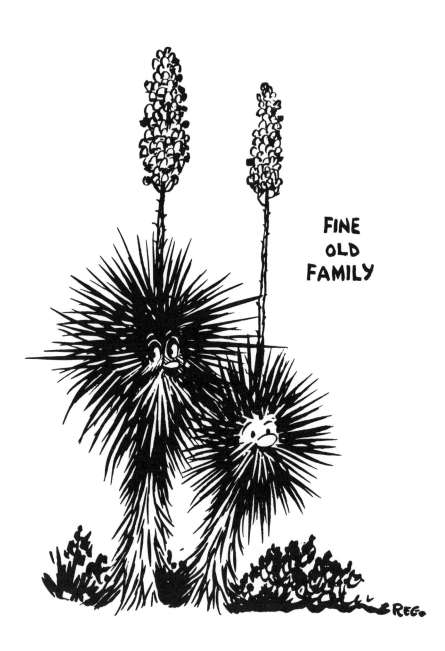

FINE
OLD
FAMILY

# YUCCA

The Yucca is no relative of the Cactus. It is a member of the enormous lily family — a family which includes the ordinary garden variety of lilies and their country cousins, the onion and garlic. The Yucca is, therefore, a sort of great uncle of the onion you ate last night. Burp.

"Spanish Dagger" or "Spanish Bayonet" — both names are familiar aliases of the Yucca (pronounced YUCK-uh). The Yucca is one of the finest old families of the west — when the Indians got here they found Yucca already established. It grows, not alone in the cactus belt, but throughout the west. The Prickly Pear is probably the only desert plant whose range is more wide-spread.

A Yucca is seldom taller than a man. With its shaggy trunk, topped by a rosette of fresh green leaves, the Yucca looks like a miniature palm tree. The sharp pointed leaves, which are about the same width and length as an army sword, earn it the popular "Spanish Dagger" or "Bayonet" titles.

# YUCCA AND MOTH

Each species of Yucca is dependent on a particular kind of moth for its very life. Yucca pollen is too heavy to be blown from plant to plant by the wind, so the moth steps in to do the job. The moth collects a ball of pollen from one flower and crams it into the flower of another Yucca; then it crawls down the side of the flower, punctures it near the base and inserts its egg. The flower, thus fertilized, gives way to the fruit — and the moth egg hatches a li'l Yucca worm. They start life together all over again. Without the moth to fertilize it, no seed would develop, and the Yucca would die out — if the plant were not fertilized, there would be no fruit in which the egg could incubate, and the moth would die out. Each of the 30 varieties of Yucca has its own particular moth which (with perhaps one or two exceptions) will have nothing to do with any other species of Yucca.

The blossom of the Yucca is a large bouquet of cream-white flowers clustered on a stalk which reaches two to six feet above the plant. From a distance the creamy clusters amid the green foliage look like grazing sheep. The Yucca blossom is New Mexico's state flower.

JOSHUA

# JOSHUA TREE

Imagine a lily as big as a tree — that is the Joshua Tree — grand high mogul of all the desert Yuccas. With its trunk and hairy, twisted arms, the Joshua looks not unlike some kind of tree-Cholla cactus. Joshua Trees grow as tall as 35 feet, with fistfulls of green, pointed dagger-leaves held high by the twisting arms. The arms are covered by a mat of brown "hair" — dead leaves of past growth.

The Joshua in bloom is a real show, with the flowering stalks clutched above each bristling fist.

North of Indio, in the Mohave desert of California, is Joshua Tree National Monument, established to preserve a vast area where the plant thrives. One of the finest forests of Joshuas is located not far from the shores of Lake Mead, 100 miles east of Boulder Dam, in Arizona — the forest extends for 30 miles.

JOSHUA TREES
REACH
ENORMOUS
SIZE

# SOTOL

Unless it is blooming, you'd probably ride past the Sotol and mistake it for a Spanish Dagger. In fact, they are constructed almost identically and the Sotol, too, is a member of the Lily family. But, whereas the leaves of a Yucca have wicked pointed tips, the end of a Sotol leaf is frayed. Sotol leaves are not defenseless, however — they are barbed along both edges, like a double edged band saw.

The Sotol (SOH-tole) sends up a flower stalk like the Yucca, but the effect is different. Instead of a cluster of white bell-shaped flowers, the Sotol stem is topped by a huge swab that resembles the ramrod used in an ancient cannon. The swab is made up of tightly packed, minute blossoms, each a fiftieth the size of a single flower from a Yucca cluster. Some of these Sotol swabs reach enormous size — we've seen 'em seven or eight feet long.

I MAY BE FRAYED, BUT I AIN'T SCAIRT.

# PREHISTORIC "RAW MATERIALS"

Modern nations war over oil and rubber and hemp. In the life of prehistoric peoples of the Southwest — even of Indians of not so long ago — the Desert lilies were as important as those present day raw materials. Products of the Yucca and Sotol were found in every hut — or cave — or cliff dwelling. Tough fibrous leaves of the Yucca — or those of the Sotol, stripped of their saw-edges — were the hemp of the ancients. They were not only used in making rope and twine, but were included in parts of every scanty wardrobe. Most of the prehistoric sandals were made from Sotol leaves. They were made into mats — and woven into baskets, they were indispensable in the household. The Indian basket you buy today will probablyl be made, in large part, from Yucca leaves.

Indians used to roast and eat the juicy center portions of the Sotol trunk — and Western cattlemen chop up Sotol and Yucca as an emergency fodder during drouths. Pioneers called the Yucca "soap weed" — the roots provide an excellent "soap" that Indians have long prized as a shampoo.

MODERN
INDIAN
BASKETS

REC—

# THE CENTURY PLANT

It seems that nearly every plant on the desert is forever being mistaken for some other plant. The Century Plant is confused with the Yucca, though it's easy to tell 'em apart. The Century Plant rosette grows right on the ground — the leaves are broad as your hand, with vicious jagged edged. It looks like an artichoke bud magnified to fill the whole table.

The principal reason for confusing the Century Plant with the Yucca is that they both send up blossoms on a stalk. The Century Plant lives 10 to 75 years (not a century) and blooms only once in its life time. After spending its life getting ready to bloom, the plant wastes no time once it gets started. It sends up the stalk, which starts out looking like an overgrown shoot of asparagus, and grows as much as a foot a day until it is 15 to 30 feet high. You can almost SEE th' dern thing grow. The pale-yellow flowers form in clusters on short stems branching from the top of the enormous stalk. The Century Plant pours everything into this one splurge in the "stalk market". Its reserve supply of sap is all used up — and the plant shrivels and expires.

BUDDING
FLOWER
STALK

LIKE A PIECE
OF ASPARAGUS
STUCK IN
AN
ARTICHOKE

# AGAVE, MAGUEY, MESCAL

"Agave", "maguey" and "mescal" are other names by which the Century Plant is known in Old Mexico. They're pronounced ah-GAH-vy, m'GAY and mace-KAL. In Mexico the Century Plant is commercially grown on a large scale for the sap, which is concocted into various potent drinks. Pulque (POOL-kay), tequila (tay-KEEL-ah), and mescal are among the popular beverages fermented or distilled from maguey juice. They gained great popularity along the border in Prohibition days. Tequila connoisseurs alternate each gulp of the "firewater" with a pinch of table salt — like green apples.

The Indians used to consider the bud of a Century Plant flower-stalk one of their prime delicacies. They would cut it out of the plant just as the tip of the bud appeared above the leaves of the plant, and cook it, with others they had gathered, in a primitive "barbecue pit" of hot stones covered with earth. The result was a dish fit for a king — a golden brown goo, like sugared sweet potatoes baked to a mush.

-WITH SALT,
LIKE
GREEN APPLES

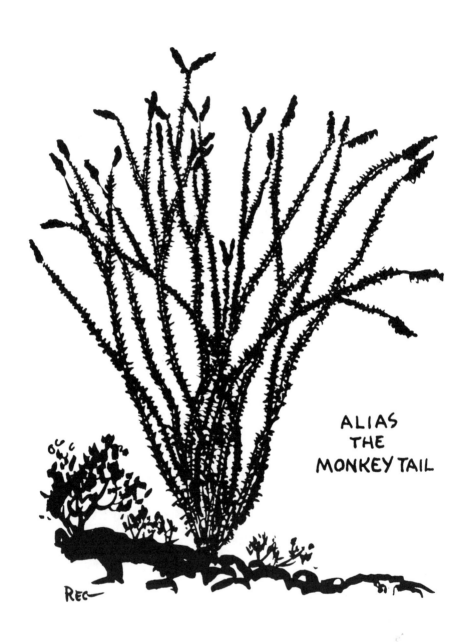

ALIAS
THE
MONKEY TAIL

# THE OCOTILLO

The Ocotillo (oh-koh-TEE-yo) is a NOTHIN'. You'll hear it called a "Monkey Tail Cactus", but it's not a cactus. And it's not a lily. It's not closely related to any other plant of the Southwest desert. South of California, in old Mexico, it has one kin, the Boogum Tree, which is an even stranger plant. These two belong to a scanty family which the botany boys (in desperation) named "Fouquieriaceae" — whatever that means. To ordinary folks the Ocotillo has more aliases than a check artist. Besides "monkey tail" it is known as "candlewood", "coach whip", "Jacob's staff", etc.

The Ocotillo is one of the strangest, most beautiful of all the strange and beautiful plants on the desert. Once you have seen it, you will never mistake an Ocotillo for anything else. Each plant is a spray of spindly stems, "monkey tails", 10 to 20 feet long—bound tightly together at the base and fanning upward like a peacock's tail. In the spring a flaming scarlet flower blazes from the tip of every stem. The flower is actually a cluster of tiny red bells — a cluster the size of a blow torch flame — and bright as a debutante's finger-nails. Find a whole mountainside covered with these scarlet-tipped fans, and you've really got somethin' for your memory book.

DESERT FAN

NAKED
IN DRY
WEATHER

# ON AGAIN, OFF AGAIN

The Ocotillo puts on a raincoat in wet weather — and goes naked when it's dry. The long stems of the plant are lined, top to bottom, with cruel thorns. Following a rain, leaves crop out in little bunches around each thorn, completely covering the stem with a feathery coat of brilliant green. As soon as dry weather comes again, the Ocotillo drops all these leaves to keep 'em from giving away any precious moisture by evaporation.

The Ocotillo manufactures its own thorns — makes 'em out of leaves. The new growth of the plant each year has no thorns — only leaves. When these leaves dry up and fall off, their stems turn into the formidable spikes which line the branch.

Mexicans chop off Ocotillo stalks, push 'em into the ground, close together, and use 'em for fences. Usually the fence takes root and continues to live and bloom.

Very loosely translated from the Spanish, Ocotillo means "little pine knot". Dead Ocotillo sticks are heavily laden with resin. Indians used to make 'em into bundles for torches.

OCOTILLO
BLOSSOMS

# THE BOOGUM TREE

The Boogum (BOO-jum) Tree is the COCKEYEDEST creation of nature. It resembles something you dream about after a hearty midnight supper of cold lobster — something a surrealist might figure out in one of his wilder moments. The only thing that could look remotely like it would be an enormous white radish planted upside down, tapering end sticking straight up, and scrawny little branches sprouting where the radish roots would be. If that isn't clear to you, don't worry about it — it won't be very clear to you even after you see it. You probably won't believe it anyway.

The Boogum Tree is a native of Old Mexico, growing south of California in the Mexican state of Baja California. But it is becoming one of the most popular additions to Southwest cactus gardens — so you'll probably see it when you come West.

91

# THE CHAPARRAL

In and around the cacti and other odd desert plants billows the chaparral — the brush — a sea of low trees and bushes. Try riding horseback for half a day through this growth, and you will be painfully convinced tha cowboys do not wear those big flapping leather "chaps" just to look romantic. If a cow puncher without chaps tried to follow a wild cow through the chaparral, he would be undressed in about ten jumps. For desert bushes and trees are not namby-pamby things. Most of 'em have more thorns than leaves.

But don't get the idea that desert trees are villains They have all been life-long friends of the desert dwellers, man and beast. They are true members of the desert family, possessing that quality, common to all plants in the cactus belt of being able to survive and thrive on a minimum of moisture.

SEA OF FOLIAGE

# THE PALO VERDE

The Palo Verde is probably the greenest tree in the world — a claim you'd hardly expect to be made for a desert plant. Other trees — evergreen trees of the forest, or the ordinary trees in your yard at home — are not green at all. They're brown. Only their leaves or needles are green. But the Palo Verde is really green. The trunk, every limb, every twig, even the thorns — all are as green as a green apple. "Verde", means "green" in Spanish. "Palo Verde" (pal-oh-VAIR-day), means "green stick".

The Palo Verde is constructed somewhat along the lines of an apple tree — short of trunk, wide spreading branches, etc. But there the resemblance ends. It has minute leaves, but they are a luxury reserved only for rainy seasons. Like the Ocotillo, it sheds its leaves during dry weather — which is most of the time.

When the Palo Verdes bloom, in April or May, they set the whole landscape afire. It is nothing short of a "spectacle". Each tree becomes a mass of lacy lemon-yellow — an effect produced by millions of tiny flowers.

PALO VERDE IN BLOOM —

TOUGH OL'
WESTERNER

# MESQUITE

Mesquite (m'SKEET) is a hard, gruff ol' boy, a true son of the West — a character in every Western novel. He is really a friendly cuss, once y' get to know him, but he's tough as they come. He's a great pal o' Palo Verde — you often see 'em hanging out together in desert arroyos. Peach Tree, Texas, was so named because tenderfoot land-promoters from the North thought the Mesquites were unpruned peach trees — and that's just what the Mesquite tree looks like. Mesquite is gray-brown of bark, amply supplied with thorns. Even a tender shoot, springing from the ground, is armed with long straight spikes. The tiny, dull-green leaflets of the Mesquite, set in pairs along their stem, look a lot like those of the common Locust tree.

Mesquite wood is dark red-brown, mahogany-hard and very heavy. It has always been the favorite firewood of the desert — the hard wood burns down to fine, long-lasting coals. You can't keep it a secret if you're burning Mesquite — it gives off a peculiar aroma that penetrates the whole countryside. (It also penetrates your hair, your clothes and the food you're cooking.) The wood has found its way into the construction of many a primitive dwelling — of the Indians and White pioneers. It was a natural for fence posts, when barbed wire came along, and the pioneers found the hard wood perfect for tool handles, etc.

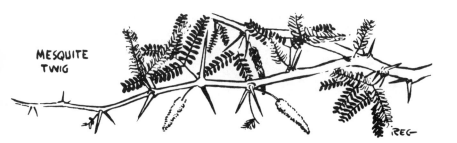

MESQUITE
TWIG

# MESQUITE BEANS

The two principal kinds of Mesquite that grow in the desert may be told apart by their bean pods. The "screwbean" Mesquite pod is rolled up into a tight coil. The whole coil is smaller than a cigarette. The pods are in clusters, as many as two dozen to the bunch.

The "Honey" Mesquite bean grows in a long, flat pod, the size and shape of string beans, about a dozen beans to the pod. The dry pods are almost white (as are the Screwbeans) and the beans themselves are very sweet. Pleasant tasting even to the human palate, the Mesquite bean is a delicacy to nearly every animal of the desert. Cattle thrive on 'em — all desert rodents dote on 'em — even Coyotes nibble the beans from low hanging pods. The Indians grind 'em into flour.

The bloom of the Mesquite is a little tassel, made up of many minute flowers. White at first, the tassel turns yellow before it drops off. Bees go for Mesquite flowers in a big way — and the honey manufactured from them is unbeatable.

THE TOUGHEST LI'L
TOUGH GUY

# IRONWOOD

Ironwood is not recommended for ordinary after-dinner whittling—
it is even harder than the name suggests, and don't try to make a raft
out of Ironwood — it is so heavy it won't float. The stuff is practically
everlasting — a dead stump will lie for decades, half buried in a desert
wash, and remain apparently just as solid and sound as ever. Ironwood
is so hard it has proven almost useless to desert dwellers — they could
never find tools tough enough to work on it. The wood polishes beauti-
fully for small novelties. It is heavy enough for paper-weights — and
so hard that it makes a satisfactory ash tray.

Desert Ironwood is related to the Mesquite and Palo Verde — all
are members of the Pea family. That's right, they're cousins of the little
ol' garden Pea that comes in cans. Ironwood looks quite a lot like Mesquite, too. It has the same Locust-type double leaflets, but the thorns
are heavier and curved. The bark is a little more gray — and the pods
have dark round "peas", instead of the Mesquite's lighter, flat "beans".
Ironwood flowers are decidedly different. Instead of tassels, the half-
inch blossoms form in little purple bouquets.

CATCLAW

HOW
MISTLETOE
GETS ITS
START

REC-

CRUCIFIXION
THORN

# THE CATCLAW

The Catclaw is another rugged member of the Pea family cousin of the Mesquite and Ironwood, which gets its name (as you have probably figured out) from the shape of its thorns — though sometimes they reach a size that looks more like tiger's claws. The average Catclaw is a straggling shrub, seldom taller than a man. Its bean pods are twisted like pieces of too-done bacon — sometimes there'll be only one seed to the pod.

# HANGER-ON

If someone tells you that Mesquite, Ironwood and Catclaw have little red berries and waxy, flat leaves, don't be too quick to call him a liar. He will have seen the Mesquite Mistletoe that attaches itself to all these plants; like "friends" to a winning candidate. This tough desert hanger-on is not as attractive as your delicate "kiss-bait" mistletoe. Birds like its berries — but they are sticky. After a feast, the bird flies to a neighboring tree to wipe its gummed-up beak — the berries hang onto the bark and start growing.

# CRUCIFIXION THORN

Here's a shrub that's so thorny it has thorns on its thorns. In fact, its Latin name, Holacantha, means, "all thorn". Which is 100% correct. It doesn't even have leaves — only small scales which fall off in dry weather. Every little branch is a cruelly pointed spur, sharp as a gamecock's gaff. The Crucifixion-thorn attains small-tree size, as much as 12 feet tall. It grows in southern Arizona and California, and in Sonora, Mexico.

# THE CREOSOTE BUSH

The rich green leaves of the Creosote Bush (often called "Grease-wood") are never disturbed by grazing cattle. It is one of the few desert plants which does not depend on thorns for protection. It just tastes so bad that the animals will have nothing to do with it. The oil-filled leaves shining as though they had just been painted with green lacquer, all grow at the ends of the spindly branches. "Greasewood" is the "parsley" of the Cactus Belt, garnishing the desert spaces around the larger thorny plants and softening harsh outlines of the rocky terrain with its green filigree. It is particularly thick in regions where the Giant Saguaro grows.

DESERT "PARSLEY"

REG

ADVICE—
**LOOK** BEFORE YOU **SIT!**

# FATHERLY ADVICE

If it annoys you to read "do's and don't", you can skip this page — but don't blame us if you get stuck. Your enjoyment of the desert will be increased if you will observe a few simple rules.

Take plenty of water and extra gas if you leave the main roads. There is no need to drive on unmarked trails into isolated desert areas — there are lots of good roads through splendid cactus country. (See map, pp. 68-69) Don't destroy ANY cactus — it may have taken a century to grow it. Don't try to carry away cacti — reasons: thorny small ones may injure you; you'll find larger ones too heavy to lift after you've pushed them over; some states have fines as high as $300 for each plant disturbed without permission of authorities. Be careful what you touch — if you get "attached" to a Cholla, use a stick to pry it loose; remove remaining stickers with tweezers. If you walk in your sleep, keep your shoes on. Don't spread your bed roll in those nice smooth sandy washes — a distant thunderstorm may send a torrent of water rushing down without warning — and it's unhealthy to wake up under several feet of water.

Now, hop to it, m'friend — you'll love the desert if you don't get stuck on it!

107